CW00687654

BANG
SAID
THE GUN

Bang Said The Gun is a registered trademark of Bang Said The Gun Limited.
Selection copyright © 2013 Bang Said The Gun Limited.
Introduction copyright © 2013 Ian McMillan
Copyright of individual poems rests with the individual poets

The authors and editors assert their moral right under the Copyright,
Designs and Patents Act 1988 to be identified as the authors of this work

All rights reserved. No part of this publication may be reproduced, stored in
a retrieval system, or transmitted, in any form or by any means without the
prior written consent of Burning Eye Books, nor be otherwise circulated in
any form of binding or cover other than that in which it is published and
without a similar condition being imposed on the subsequent purchaser.

Dear Gunslingers,
It wouldn't be possible without you.

Thank you.

CONTENTS

INTRODUCTION
10
ROB AUTON
14
NIA BARGE
22
JO BELL
26
TIM CLARE
30
DANIEL COCKRILL
36
INUA ELLAMS
40

MARTIN GALTON
48
SALENA GODDEN
60
MATT HARVEY
70
PETER HAYHOE
76
JOHN HEGLEY
82
EMMA JONES
86
MURRRAY LACHLAN YOUNG
90
ELVIS McGONAGALL
92
IAN McMILLAN
102

HOLLIE McNISH
104
ADRIAN MEALING
110
MOLLY NAYLOR
112
JOHN OSBORNE
114
POLARBEAR
118
KATE TEMPEST
120
BYRON VINCENT
126
DAVE VINEY
132
LUKE WRIGHT
136

INTRODUCTION

Some of the first poetry gigs I ever did were in pub rooms; upstairs, or off the main bar, or round the back in an annexe you reached from the car park. The Red Deer, The Sun Inn, The George and Dragon, The Rockingham Arms. The rooms felt full of excitement, full of a kind of rough theatre that meant on a good night you couldn't hear yourself read for the laughter and applause and on a bad night you could hear your voice echoing round the room as someone crunched a crisp and the darts team downstairs cheered a double top. Somehow it felt that these rooms were just the right place for poetry to be heard and seen.

And Bang Said the Gun carries on this magnificent tradition at The Roebuck; I did a gig there last year and arrived early, as I always do, and I watched as the room was transformed from an ordinary space above a bar to a palace of literary delight. The audience were given all kinds of things to make noise with and they were encouraged, before the show began, to make as much noise as they possibly could.

Now, I've done lots of gigs in all kinds of settings but I have to admit that, as the noise grew and grew until it nudged the cacophony barrier and then shattered it, I was a little nervous. I clutched my little poetry pamphlets like lifebelts. I stood up to read after a thundering welcome that my family could hear back home in Barnsley.

IAN McMILLAN

And then the Bang Said the Gun Miracle happened: the audience went quiet and listened. If listening is an art, Bang Said the Gun has perfected it, made masterpieces of it. This is creative listening, listening that becomes part of the poem, almost redrafts it as it hangs in the air.

So welcome to this, the Bang Said the Gun Anthology; in here you'll find poems by lots of people who've climbed those steps to that upper room and experienced the sublime delight of the BSTG Vortex. And maybe, in these terrible times, this is a model for a direction that spoken word can take: the room full of listeners, the poet on the stage, the whole event becoming greater than the sum of its parts: words as theatre, as opera, as art.

One of the first poetry readings I ever saw was at The Brewery Tap in Doncaster in, I think, 1973. I took my girlfriend along to impress her. The poets were The Liverpool Poets: Henri, McGough and Patten. Adrian Henri stood up, looked around the crowded-to-bursting room and said 'Once an alehouse poet, always an alehouse poet'. Bang Said the Gun carries on the tradition of the alehouse poet and takes it to new places. Enjoy!

And that girlfriend has been my wife for 34 years: the power of pub poetry!

1906 Charlie Chaplin performs at the Roebuck

1956 Martin Galton born on a farm in South Ockendon, Essex

1973 Daniel Cockrill born in the back of his Dad's taxi

1980 Peter Hayhoe born at his Mum's house in Penge

2001 BSTG move to Old Coffee House Soho

2000 Peter still living with his mum

1999 Dan and Martin appear on BBC Radio

1999 Wheatsheaf remove stage and replace it with a pool table

1998 first BSTG gig at Wheatsheaf, London

2001 Martin uses the words 'Stand Up Poetry' to describe BSTG

2002 Dan banned by BBC for swearing live on air

2004 BSTG appear at Bowery Club New York

2007 Dan has first collection of poems published: 'Pie and Papier Mâché'

2012 10 million viewers watch Bang short films on Channel 4

2011 Oxford University announce that BSTG is the 'Death of Poetry'

2011 Peter joins BANG team. Still lives with his mum

2011 BSTG perform at Edinburgh Festival (20 x 5 star reviews – that is a 100 star show)

2010 Woman from number 36 makes first complaint about the noise at a poetry event

2012 Sky TV offer BSTG half million pounds to make Bang TV

2012 Roger McGough and Andrew Motion appear at BSTG

2012 BSTG rock Ledbury Poetry Festival

2012 BSTG walk away from Sky TV deal

1982 Rob Auton born in Spike Milligan's sock drawer

1990 Dan writes his first poem entitled 'Bath Bomb'

1991 Sarah Redington born in a huge fairytale kingdom called Love

1992 Dan sees John Hegley on television. Writes a few more poems

1994 Rock Writers formed. Dan performs live for the first time

1998 Martin draws Bang Logo and creates BSTG

1996 Martin sees Dan perform live in a cave. Martin decides he wants to perform poetry in a cave

1996 Dan wins Poetry competition with his poem 'The Scream'

1996 Dan sees Adrian Mitchell live. Decides he definitely wants to be a poet

2008 first gig at the Roebuck (the home of BSTG)

2009 First shaker introduced

2009 World famous Tequila Shot Open mic spot

2010 Martin writes 'Rude Bastard'

2010 BSTG goes weekly

2010 Tequila Shot is replaced with RAW MEAT STEW GOLDEN GUN AWARD

2010 John Hegley, Ian McMillan, Murray Lachlan Young, Kate Tempest appear at BSTG

2010 Sarah joins BANG team

2010 2 people who don't like poetry fall in love at BSTG

2012 Rob Auton performs Yellow Show at Edinburgh Festival to critical acclaim

2013 Rob publishes his first collection of poems 'In Heaven The Onions Make You Laugh'

2013 BSTG launches BANG TV channel on You Tube

2013 BSTG Anthology published

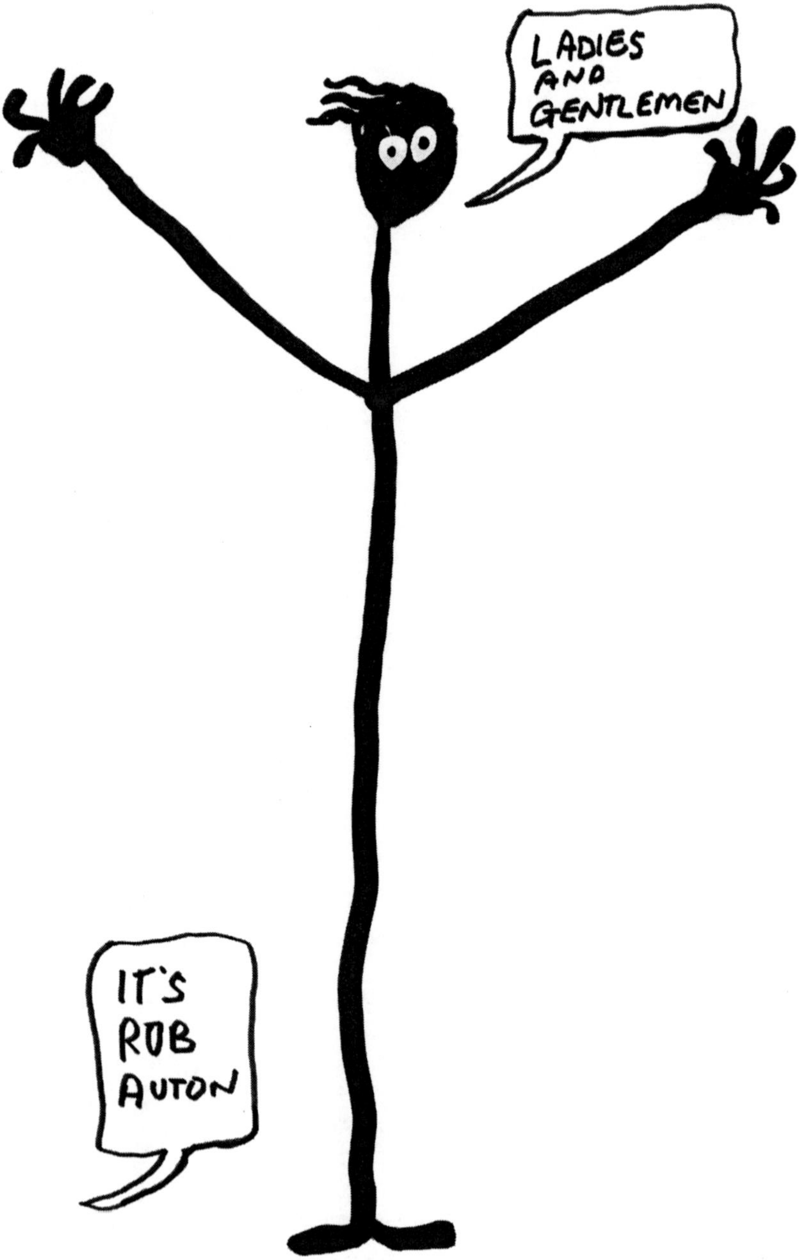
LADIES AND GENTLEMEN
IT'S ROB AUTON

FATHER AND SON

If I have a son
His name will be Dad
After my Dad, and his Dad, and his Dad, and his Dad, and his Dad
At the hospital I will introduce Dad to my Mum
Mum this is Dad, your Grandson
Don't cry Dad, it's Mum, your Grandma
On Christmas Eve I will say to him
You better get to bed soon Dad or Father Christmas won't come
And he will be confused but not as confused as me
As he grows up other children will call him by his name
and my son will become the father figure of the playground
PASS ME THE BALL DAD
My Mum said you can come round to my house for tea tonight Dad
At morning registration his teacher will call him by his name
in a voice of complete and utter tenderness
Dad

CARSPOTTER

I spot cars
I am a carspotter
I stand on the side of the road and write down number plates
If it's a busy road I don't write down the number plate
I just say
There's one
There's one
There's one
If the roads are really busy I say
There's two
There's two
There's two
Sometimes if the roads are really, really busy
I don't even say there's two
I just say YES
Yes
Yes
Yes
When I was little my parents took me on holiday to the M1
I am a carspotter, my favourite type of jam is traffic
I like to sit in parks that have tarmac instead of grass and cars instead of trees

FOOTBALLER'S LIFE FOR ME

I work in an art supplies shop
I get paid £250,000 a week
Crowds of screaming fans gather at the windows of the shop
Wearing replicas of my staff T-shirt that says STAFF on the back.
They cheer me on with my daily tasks through chant and song
Stack those paint pots, stack those paint pots, stack those paint pots and
sell them
Stack those paint pots and sell them

If I sell a particularly expensive set of oil paints the cheers can be heard right
across Soho
Young children copy my unique method of stocktaking masking tape and rival
art shops bid to get me on their books of watercolour paper

The injuries I suffer at work such as paper cuts from cardboard boxes
Are dealt with on the spot by the staff physio
Are you sure that you can continue to work today Rob? Asks the physio
Yes I can continue I reply, to the delight of my screaming fans at the window

TV stations fight for the rights to televise footage from the shops CCTV
cameras
So the nation can see how I collapse a cardboard box or inform a customer
Yes Madam, I'm sorry, these are the only colours of pencil sharpeners
that we sell

POEM ABOUT A KETTLE

(Written when listening to a lot of Leonard Cohen)

I filled my kettle with tears
The tears I stole from your eyes when you weren't looking.
Clicked it on to boil
After a minute I could hear your distant weeping
With the heat came the cries
Before long the kitchen was full of bubbling screams
The kettle peaked, extinguishing the little light it had
I poured your sorrow onto the teabag of my life
And drank the sadness of your being

KEY

As he got up to leave the train
A small gold key fell from his pocket
I pick it up, Sorry, is this yours?
He looked at the key Oh thanks
No expression or maybe that was his happy face
His *Oh my God I can't believe I nearly lost that key* face
I began to imagine what the small gold key was for
A window he hated opening
An empty safe
Or maybe it was a key he had been trying to lose
Dropping it again and again
People forever picking it up and giving it back to him
If I hadn't picked it up I might have made his day

YELLOW SUPERMARKET

Take a melon from the shelf take a melon for yourself
Take a lemon from the shelf take a lemon for yourself
Put the lemon and the melon in a trolley for yourself
Take bananas from the shelf take bananas for yourself
Tin of sweetcorn from the shelf tin of sweetcorn for yourself
Ignore the fact that there's a green giant on the tin
He may be green and he may also be a giant but he would be nothing without
the sweetcorn
Yellow peppers from the shelf in a trolley for yourself
Take a grapefruit from the shelf take a grapefruit for yourself
Grapefruit sounds like great fruit, that's because that is what it is
Why is a grapefruit called a grapefruit? There is already a fruit called a grape
And a grapefruit looks nothing like the grape that's a fruit

Take a pineapple from the shelf take a pineapple for yourself
It may look brown on the outside
But fruit is just like humans
It's what's on the inside that counts
Not in the case of the pink grapefruit

The bottom of your trolley's getting yellow
The bottom of your trolley's getting yellow
Lower your chin down to your shopping and think of each product
as a buttercup
IS YOUR CHIN YELLOW? Do you like SHOPPING?
You can't see because mirrors are quite rare in supermarkets

Don't take an apple from the shelf don't take an apple for yourself
Not even Golden Delicious
Don't be fooled into thinking they are yellow by the name
They are golden by the name and gold is not the same

ROB AUTON

Move from fruit and veg down to dairy it is where you'll find the cheese
So much yellow in the cheese so much yellow you're so pleased
Take some cheddar from the shelf
Take some edam from the shelf
Take some stilton from the shelf
Take some stilton for yourself
Take away the stilton it has green contained in it

Margerine and butter from the shelf for your self
Yellow jumping out at you from shelf to yourself
You start to run down the aisles grabbing all that shines
Grab some Marmite for the lid
Grab some Marmite you just did, eat the lid
Yellow plastic in your teeth yellow plastic in your teeth
Yellow plastic in your teeth this does mean that you're a thief
A voice comes over the tannoy system
"Security please go to the cereal aisle where a man is attempting to make
a fort out of Shredded Wheat boxes, Lemon Fresh Domestos bottles and
pineapple chunks."

I am in my fort they cannot get me
I have got supplies for one year maybe three
Peanut M&Ms, Jelly Tots, Lemon Puffs
Orangina, Lemon Tarts, Barley Water, Rubber Gloves

The security staff knock down my fort
I sit surrounded in colour

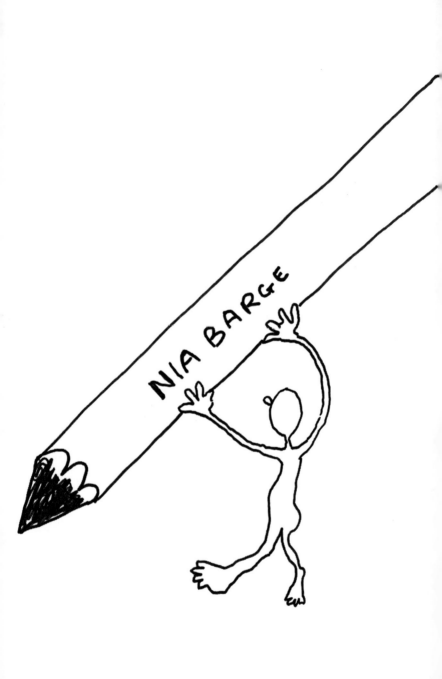

DISFIGURED LIMBS

This might be the realest piece I ever wrote
My thank you note
My transcription of gratitude depicted and engraved in the skins of my
next of kin
This is my repentance.
My wrong doings have indebted and paid through the reassurance of my loved
ones content
This is an acknowledgment of my family's disfigured limbs

My mother, has hope for hands
So imagine every time she touched my face it was hope that landed
Imagine that her fingers were replaced by faith and promise took over the palm
of her hand
So when she made a fist she was promising to have faith in all that my hopes
could imagine
And when her fingers opened up, curled from the palm of her hand
Her hope was that my faith would find me in a promised land
Mom, I now understand your disfigured hands

This is for my Dad, for being there
For being the first man to believe in me
For being magical, laughable, for having motivation in place of his clavicle
For having a chest constructed from pieces of struggle
Working doubles, 18 hour shifts, selling beepers and purses, hustling
Daddy, I know what your disfigured body is for
Why instead of a heart your passion beats
Why you have determination in place of your feet.
It's because your lungs were replaced by resilience and humility.
So you breathe in success and you blow out defeat
Because your shoulders were amputated and made place holders for my
courage to grow
I'm sure of it
I got here because my footprints are engraved in your back.

Sketched in permanent ink
Where my toes have tried to spell out thank you in an indelible speech
And if I succeed, it will be because your body was mutated and transformed into my opportunity
And this might be the realest piece I ever wrote but
I didn't write it for me

Or the need to impress with the metaphorical weight I could bench press
I'd strip the weight and only raise the bar
I'd spit this poem from afar and hope its message elevated high enough to tell my sisters...
Aim for the stars
And to use my shoulders, if they're ever in danger of hovering over and shying away from their dreams
I'd transfer my eyes for all my cousins to see
Disfigure my body leave my skin on the streets broken, torn and tattered
Relocate my bones so they'd be able to hold onto your fears so you can let go
Of hesitation, doubt, insecurity
And grip the sheets of life wholly, hungry, boldly, proudly
This is why I disfigured my body

This is promise sealed in a bottle sent out to sea
I'll be pushing as long as my heart beats
This is gratitude for my grandparents that graciously prayed for me
This is my consent for you to use my limbs to transcend mediocrity
This is my hope, my thank you note
Maybe the realest piece I ever wrote

This is for my nephew and my niece.
I've got open palms to help guide you along
I've got hope for hands that will hoist you up to stand
I'll wrap my hope around your potential and we'll walk hand in hand
I need you to know you have potential for hands
And there is room on my back if you ever need a place to stand

~~JOKING~~

~~JOBURG~~

~~JOVIAL~~

JO BELL

COMING

So many different ways; why not?
There would be, doing what
comes naturally.

There are the men who scream and groan,
who bite their lip, forgetting you entirely;
oddly flattering.

Some stare into your eyes
so you can see them shudder at the climax
as if offered tripe.

Others grasp you by the throat
to choke off some imaginary love
or maybe you.

One laughed hysterically every time
and slapped his thigh if any hands were free
which was offputting.

Some sigh, relieved
as if they've just remembered what they came in for
or broken wind.

Some are shocked, as if the whole thing took them by surprise;
I'm terribly sorry, I don't quite know what happened there.
And some just stop.

URBAN MERMAID

Surfacing at 1am, she's taken by surprise.
Last time she came this far inland
it was all hedge and larksong.

The factories have been and gone, their poisons
spent. The basin is a citied silence.
Leaking lock gates, lamplight drunks.

The lamplight drunk is not at all surprised.
He understands that she has lost her way.
He has faith in fairy tales.

They both lament the passing of lost loves.
She combs the condoms from her hair.
He sits on a bin and sings to her.

He slouches into sleep; she slips into the lock
but on the coping stones she leaves a shell
so he can hear the sea;

takes in return his can of Special Brew.
She holds it to her ear sometimes, and listens to
the roaring of the trains at platform 2.

OIKS

The walk may be Churchillian,
chin in and belly first:
you don't fool me.
I've seen you fucking in the shallows,
shouting like a bus-stop drunk at 3am.
You're drab and scrawny TWOCkers
cruising for an open door;
on patrol and on the ante,
cocky as the Little Boats,
common as muck.

Over here lads, there's some bird
with a sandwich.
Don't give us plate-scraped lettuce,
couscous, scraps of rocket for fuck's sake;
we want bread
and none of your granary shit.
What do we want?
Bread.
When do we want it?
Now, and now, and now.

The shop-bought stripe of colour
on each wing, cheap as Primark,
the old-fashioned gang rape every spring;
She's down, get in.

TIM CLARE

NOAH'S ARK & GRILL

Come, traveller, to a simpler time
Where dirty kitchens aren't a crime
And diarrhoea flows like wine
It's Noah's Ark & Grill

The walls have ears – so does the veal
There's elbow grease in every meal
The champagne's fake, the hooves are real
At Noah's Ark & Grill

The safety's off in this cabana
Floor tiles smeared in brown… banana
Scrub the dishes? Eh! Mañana!
Noah's Ark & Grill

The Ark & Grill's a thrifty treat
Each meal is a surprise
Gorillas in the mystery meat
Free willy in the pies

Our presence takes a drastic toll on
Local pets: they've all been stolen
Gingivitis? Spastic colon?
Roll on Noah's Ark & Grill

Come feast your deviated septums
On our deep-fried walrus rectums
Hygiene guidelines? We reject 'em!
Make sure you've had your injections
Noah's Ark & Grill

Wake up and smell the Ark & Grill
The crackle of pork taint
Leaves critics stricken, stark and ill
Cos haute cuisine it ain't

The lamb chops taste of duffel coat
The prime ribs taste of murder
We use parts of the buffalo
The Navajo ain't heard of

Fresh flesh for every nature lover!
Pasties filled by Noah's brother
Contents from the bin marked 'other'
Noah's Ark & Grill

Punters puce with streptococci
Puke green like a backwards Popeye
Suicidal? Please, drop by to
Noah's Ark & Grill

Dysentery? This century?
The peasants are delighted!
Your bum's a penitentiary
And everyone's invited

The lawsuits come in two-by-two
The crow spines come in baskets
The dolphin pie is tuna-safe
If you need proof… just ask it
[dolphin noise] What's that Flipper?
You can't understand why God doesn't end your suffering?

We haven't lost a diner yet
The secret sauce is pure regret
Free vein in every grilled courgette
At Noah's Ark & Grill

You'd best bring an umbrella, they say
Lest some peaky fella spray stray
Chunks like an unweller Fay Wray
Lurking lawyers smell a payday
Hipsters think it's hella cray-cray
'Haters are just jealous, baby.'
Help us! Mayday!
Noah's Ark & Grill

No guts, no glory, them's the breaks
Tuck in and take your chances
A DNA test on our steaks
Reads like a list of Kung Fu stances:

Monkey, tiger, dwarf gazelle,
The bat, the crane, yes, horse as well,
Reconstituted Orson Welles
The portions swell
To caution, Hell
At Noah's Ark & Grill

The blender bletches reds and pinks
While slender wretches retch in sinks
Bacteria? You betcha. [winks]
The food chain's got some extra links
At Noah's Ark & Grill

Each Easter when we clean the floor
It looks just like a scene from Saw
Please sir, can I have some mor-
phine? Seriously. I need morphine.
Noah's Ark & Grill

The chips come with a side of flies
The wafers are communion-sized
The salmonella's unionised
At Noah's Ark & Grill

And if you feel a nagging stab
Through rolls of grey unfeeling flab
When finally you pay your tab
At Noah's Ark & Grill

Wipe off the grease, put down your knife
Remember these two rules for life:
The best things come to those who grab
Don't eat a burger with a scab

TIM CLARE

MANGO

Ian Beale eats five mangoes and tells me I have wasted my life.

'Each mango represents a father figure
who has abandoned you,' says my therapist, three days later.
'The dream is encouraging you to fulfil your potential;
like a father, the subconscious has a fondness for puns:
Man Go. Be All.'
I say: 'But it wasn't a dream.'

My therapist flips through our sessions' notes
with the slow-burning confusion of Ian Beale;
he scrunches the pages into a mango
which he throws at my head.
'I'm sorry, I can no longer treat you.'
'But Dad –'
'Stop calling me that.'

The next day I buy five mangoes
and carve them into likenesses of Ian Beale.
Each one is an improvement on the last; viewed right to left,
they depict Ian Beale gradually mutating into a mango,
the gentle eyes sealing over, the statesmanlike nose
retreating into smooth, green flesh.
'Dad,' I tell the one most like a mango,
'I still don't understand why you left.'
It listens without passing judgement.
It is the perfect father, even when I bite into its face,

even when I throw it at my father,
a man who looks like Ian Beale,
and also, strangely, a mango.

Dan Cockrill.

THERE'S A MAN ON THE ROOF OF THE WORLD

and he's dancing
he's dancing in the sky

the world's falling down
help me catch it
the world's falling down
help me hold it

I'm madly in love
I'm madly in love with the world

the world's falling down
help me catch it
the world's falling down
help me hold it
help me hold the world

we've put the world on trial
look death in the eye

I'm madly in love
I'm madly in love with the world

the world's falling down
help me catch it
the world's falling down
help me hold it

so we can dance
dance on the roof of the world
let's dance

I'm madly in love.

MARGATE IS

a long shadow
a broken window
a torn poster
a tongue-tied roller coaster

an original Turner
a single mother
a window seat that's taken
a blind Nelson

a down season grotto
a drained lido
a jellied eel
an empty shell

a tidal town
a fragile frown
things I'll never understand
a Dreamland.

WHEN MY WORLD WAS TURNED UPSIDE DOWN

Everything fell out

In the morning
I fell out of bed

My pens fell out my bag
My money fell out my pocket
My tears fell out my eyes
My thoughts fell out my ears
My anger fell out my mouth
My hate fell out my fists
My love fell out my heart
My heart fell out my chest

Luckily
You walked behind me
And picked them all up.

DIRECTIONS

– after Billy Collins

You know the wild bush at the back of the flat,
the one that scrapes the kitchen window,
the one that struggles for soil and water
and fails where the train tracks scar the ground?
And you know how if you leave the bush
and walk the stunted land, you come
to crossroads, paved just weeks ago:
hot tar over the flattened roots of trees,
and a squad of traffic lights, red-eyed now
stiff against the filth-stained fallen leaves?

And farther on, you know
the bruised allotments with the broken sheds
and if you go beyond that you hit
the first block of Thomas Street Estate?
Well, if you enter and ascend, and you
might need a running jump over
dank puddles into the shaking lift
that goes no further than the fourth floor,
you will eventually come to a rough rise
of stairs that reach without railings
the run-down roof as high as you can go
and a good place to stop.

The best time is late evening
when the moon fights through
drifts of fumes as you are walking,
and when you find an upturned bin
to sit on, you will be able to see
the smog pour across the city
and blur the shapes and tones
of things, and you will be attacked

by the symphony of tyres, airplanes,
sirens, screams, engines –
and if this is your day you might even
catch a car chase or a hear a horde
of biker boys thunder-cross a bridge.

But it is tough to speak these things
how tufts of smog enter the body
and begin to wind us down,
how the city chokes us painfully against
its chest made of secrets and fire,
how we, built of weaker things, regard
our sculpted landscape, water flowing
through pipes, the clicks of satellites
passing over clouds and the roofs
where we stand in the shudder of progress
giving ourselves to the vast outsides.

Still, text me before you set out.
Knock when you reach my door
and I will walk you as far as the tracks
with water for your travels and a hug.
I will watch after you and not turn back
to the flat till you merge
with the throngs of buses and cyclists –
heading down toward the block,
scuffing the ground with your feet.

INUA ELLAMS

ROBIN HOOD TO A FRIEND

– after John Keats

At best, you'll get a slap on the wrist.
At worst, one year. Tops. But tell me
of that night I pulled down your council
drive. You rushed out in green tights,
drinking-straw arrows, a papier-mâché
hat, tried to high-five your father who
grunted from the doorstep but wished
safe journey through the twitching broken
lights and gardens overgrown in the dim
constellation of streets we called home.

The pirate radio rapper, who rhymed
our truth, faded on the bridge we crossed
towards the chairman's house and
parked our battered Punto two doors
down from Porches, Jeeps and Benzes
laid like new shoes up the winding
drive where the doorman smiled us in
to a world of Louboutins, suits from
Savile Row and rented fancy dresses,
sequined, starched, sharp against
the best of our home made efforts.

We saw her then. Beneath a chandelier,
the chairman's niece, hostess of the house:
tiara of pale flowers, jade gown flowing,
the Maid Marian to your Hood, you said,
and when the chandeliers dimmed for
slow dances, you marched past Batman,
two Thunder Cats, a Teenage Mutant

Turtle, reached for her hand and reeled
off those lines of nice eyes, lost angels,
destiny, etc, till Buzz Lightyear called
across the falling silence to his friend
Woody who came through pools of light,
slapped off your hand, pushed against
your chest, Maid Marian laughing, tell
me was it then you made up your mind?

Or hours later when dawn's light had
snuck through curtains and you woke
to a mansion of snores, us all asleep,
the forest-flora wallpaper; chandeliers
like frozen rain, did the urban fox's yowl
strengthen your resolve and your shadow
fall across the hushed form of Marian
curled into the Sheriff, beside her purse,
beside his wallet, beside the wide open
window, was it then you asked yourself
what would Robin do?

MY FRIEND

– after Major Jackson & Mark Hole

Handcuffed, shaven headed, blinking
at bright blindings of camera flash
and snarling teeth, just shaking fists,
just the guilty-before-trial eyes of the jury,
no breeze to soothe the wailing widow
whose cries make humble her child's,
just stifling anger rising off the courtroom
guards and pews of law enforcers
leaning into the falling sudden hush
when the judge asks why did you stay
when you could have got away?
Only months before, Marcus Hollinsworth
and I sped down Main Street in the kind
of darkness thieves thank The Lord for:
soil-thick broth of bull-black shadows,
sweeping ink of shade, horned gargoyles
dribbling rain, stone creatures
on urban cliffs and us skirting curbs
on side streets, over fences, head down
running with our bag of spanners,
brass knuckles, bats and dummy guns.
Hours before, we stood at a bar
dangling the last of our shrapnel over
a barman's palms, their faded twinkles
metaphors for homes to call our own,
for white collars, steady desks, pay cheques,
and beach front holidays, faded dreams
of sunsets through palm trees, malt whiskey
on rocks and the white sails of yachts
on the horizon, endless and blue
as the rough truth of our actual collars,
these coins to drown them tonight.

What did it matter that Marcus and I
– me and my friend – had dabbled
in double dealings to make ends meet?
Or that a history of misdemeanours
hung around our names like bad clouds?
Or that we had mastered the art of cutting
corners and thumbs? Truth is I lacked
the brains, so when Marcus tugged my coat,
I followed. Outside, a ragged bunch
of down and outs haunted doorways,
loose women, couple junkies seeking change
and Marcus recounting how he'd overheard
a night guardsman brag of swapping shifts
with a dude pushing 50 and dementia,
that a cool 90k lay in the vault
but it was his birthday and his boss
could piss off. Marcus thought then
of brass knuckles, minimum effort,
maximum gain and there we were,
shape-shifters, speeding through
the night – me and my friend.
Years before, in a dark car park
a six foot tenner towered over
the trembling quiver of my frame,
punching out what little resistance
remained to get my car keys. Marcus
swung a cash register he'd just liberated
against the giant's brain, talking how us
small guys gotta stick together and I knew
I'd go with him, long as there were roads
and shoes to walk. Me and my friend?
Were there lines I would not cross for him?
You wonder if a conscience persistent

INUA ELLAMS

as a north wind tunnelled through me?
All I know is a single crow cried out
the stark nakedness of my own morality
in a graveyard of cars, a loneliness
echoed from my cracked chest
and I could not forget the rain
of coins, the scattered discs of silver light
falling with Marcus's fists just when
my last reach for breath grasped
nothing and fortune revealed its random
callous betrayal of even the most diligent
law abiding citizen. No one survives,
no one returns intact from the afterlife,
no one rises blood-encrusted in the arms
of a stranger and marches back to day jobs,
no one stands outside a shop front
with 90k in cash as a 50 year old wall
of army ex-cop muscle blocks
the struggling voice telling you to run,
save yourself, live a good life,
no one watches the clean knuckles
of a stranger punch bloody in one's honour
once again, so your Honour, why did I stay
when I could have got away?
It's simple really, he is my friend.

I know I'm not much of a looker
If I were an apple I'd be a cooker.

RUDE NATION

Have you noticed
that people push in front of you
more these days.
Rude bastards.
And people say
can I get – at the sandwich shop
not – may I have.
Rude bastards.
Then there's the people
who are infected with the
me me me virus.
Rude bastards.
And people who play their ipods
too loudly on the tube.
Rude bastards.
There's British Gas.
Rude bastards.
And BT.
Rude bastards.
All telephone sales people
who ring up just
when you've got home from work
or at the weekend
and try to sell you something
you don't bloody want.
Rude bastards.

Tall people who sit in front of you
at the cinema.
Rude bastards.
People who dawdle
on the pavement
so you can't get past.
Rude bastards.

People who want to look hard
and act hard.
Rude bastards.
Shop assistants.
Rude bastards.
Restaurants who want their table back
at half past eight.
Rude bastards.
People who text at the dinner table.
Rude bastards.
People who keep you waiting.
Rude bastards.
People who read your paper
over your shoulder.
Rude bastards.
Simon Cowell.
Rude bastard.
People who don't answer their phones.
Rude bastards.
People who stare at you on the tube
and then stare at your shoes.
Rude bastards.
People who blah on about
things they know nothing about.
Rude bastards.
People who randomly
honk their car horns.
Rude bastards.
People who drop chicken bones
on the pavement
after their KFC takeaway.
Rude bastards.
The announcer who says
mind the gap at the tube station.
Rude bastard.

There shouldn't be a gap there
in the first place.

People who send wedding lists.
Rude bastards.
People who let their babies cry
on public transport.
Rude bastards.
Jeremy Paxman,
Rude bastard.
Jeremy Clarkson.
Rude bastard.
Jeremy Kyle.
Rude bastard.
Anybody called Jeremy.
Rude bastards.
Fat people
who can't stop stuffing their faces
and expect the rest of us to fund
their gastric band operation.
Rude Bastards.
Old people.
Rude bastards.
Young people.
Rude bastards.
Birds that twitter
at 5am in the morning.
Rude bastards.
Anybody who writes comments
about my stuff on YouTube.
Rude bastards.
You lot
for staring at me.
Rude bastards.

WHY

Stanley never asks why.
Stanley is autistic and
why doesn't exist.

Most children are sponges
they need to know why.
Stanley never asks why.

Is it because the world
is difficult enough
already?

More likely
he simply doesn't know
how to ask questions.

Stanley is not curious.
Stanley never points like
an excited child would point

Shouting look Daddy look.
Stanley only points at
things that are familiar

a passing ice-cream van
a B&Q warehouse
the McDonalds sign.

Look Daddy look
the chip M.
The M for McDonalds
made out of chips.

MARTIN GALTON

Stanley never asks why.
If you never ask why
things will stay the same.
A strategy Stanley
seems to understand.

Stanley lives in a world
of DVDs, videos
and picture books.

He knows every
inch of dialogue,
every full stop
and comma

which he repeats over
and over and over
in his head.

When Stanley was younger
we read stories together.
We still do.

Stanley is now 15.
Each Peach Pear Plum is still
one of his favourites.

Ironically
it's a story
about I Spy,
a game he has no interest
in playing.

Stanley never asks why.
So I will ask why instead.
Why him?

Why does he have to struggle so much?
Why won't the fog lift
so he can see more clearly?
Why?
Stanley has no interest in why.

He has no interest in money.
He has no interest in winning.
He doesn't know how to lie.

Stanley never asks why
but he's found the answer
to a better way
of being.

MARTIN GALTON

A WEEK IN THE LIFE OF VICTOR

You were dancing
in Mum's tum.
I saw your kicks
both of us not sure
what to expect
as we headed for the unknown.

Today is Wednesday
and you are 14
and like your breakfast egg
you are sunny side up.

Yesterday was Tuesday
and you were 9
standing on the doorstep
in your new school uniform
with room to grow.

On Monday
you were 5
and 30,000 fans erupted
with ear splitting appreciation
as West Ham scored a goal.
I held you tight.

On Sunday
you were 2
catching balls
and dancing around the kitchen
like Billy Elliot.
You are still dancing –
racket in hand.

MARTIN GALTON

On Saturday
14 years ago
the midwife said
that's lucky
and I panicked
that you had nearly died.
He's still in his sac
she said
the waters haven't broken
that's rare that is –
he's been born lucky.
Well, I said,
he's got me as his Dad
of course he's lucky.
So from Mum
to midwife
to me
I held you
for the first time.
A rare orchid
as white as winter
and I looked into your
beautiful eyes
as big as the sky
and counted your toes
and wished you all the
music in the world
for you to dance
your own dance.

MARTIN GALTON

Tomorrow is Thursday.
You will shine brightly
and I will say
stop
slow down
slow
slow
slow
so I can catch my breath
hug every new memory
and say how much
I love you.

SMART ARSE

I went to an art class
And drew a conclusion
That most people there
Had no imagination

They simply drew
What they knew

I drew a blank

And when the teacher
Pointed out
The starkness
Of my markless
Piece of paper
I said

I was drawing breath

MARTIN GALTON

SALENA GODDEN'S BOOTS

I WANT LOVE

I want love
I want love all over me
I want to be on top of love
I want love to surround me
I want to be inside love
I want love to be inside me
I want to be consumed with love, by love
I want to be in love
I want love so hard that I go home early from the pub
I want to quit drinking and smoking for love
I want to quit crossing the road when its busy
I want to quit putting salt on unsalted butter because
I want to live so long so I can love this love as long as I can
I want a house built with love
I want a garden blooming with love and
I want beautiful children with all the love I have
I want children made of love, with love, for love and in love's name
I want to have so much love I reek of it, it stains my clothes
and fingers
I want love to leak from me
I want love to knot in my hair
I want love under my nails
I want to drink love
I want to eat love
I want to open the fridge and find love
I want to find love in the oven
I want to sleep with love and
I want to wake up with love
I want to hear love on the radio
I want to sing the songs of love
I want to write the words of love
I want to bathe love
I want to wash love's clothes

I want to clip love's toenails
I want to make love soup and love pie
I want to make love make love
I want to care for love in love's sickbed
I want to find the bail to get love out of jail
I want to go to prison for love
I want to die for love
I want to kill for love
I want to throw myself off a cliff for love
I want love to be like a cancer
I want to be terminally ill with love
I want to be riddled incurably with love
I want to fuck love in the arse
I want to fuck love up
I want to fuck love over
I want to fuck love, fuck love
I want to but
I can't

IMAGINE IF YOU HAD TO LICK IT

i have been doing this my whole life
when i am hungover on a tube train or a bus
i stare at the most stomach turning churning things
and this voice inside my head says
IMAGINE IF YOU HAD TO LICK IT
that man's shiny bald patch with scabby dandruff
IMAGINE IF YOU HAD TO LICK IT
3-day old vomit gone hard on the pavement
IMAGINE IF YOU HAD TO LICK IT
the zit on the girls chin opposite
IMAGINE IF YOU HAD TO LICK IT
the tip of that man's finger firmly rooted up his left nostril
IMAGINE IF YOU HAD TO LICK IT
that runny old dog shit
IMAGINE IF YOU HAD TO LICK IT
that drunk man's piss in that doorway
IMAGINE IF YOU HAD TO LICK IT
those old Chinese takeway noodles like maggots in the gutter by the bin
IMAGINE IF YOU HAD TO LICK IT
i mean lick it like you mean to clean it
IMAGINE IF YOU HAD TO LICK IT
i mean lick it like you really mean it
IMAGINE
and i don't mean the tip but with the very back of your tongue
like the place that makes you retch if you touch it with a toothbrush
IMAGINE
all the people! licking them! all of them! licking them! all of them!
IMAGINE IF YOU HAD TO LICK IT
that pigeon's stumped foot
IMAGINE IF YOU HAD TO LICK IT
that tramp's cock!

now i have been doing this all my life
i find myself staring at the ugly and rotten
the rancid putrid essence
until i gag and i am forced to look away
sure it makes the journey go faster
but it gives me something
else to be nauseous about...

A LETTER TO AN AIR STEWARDESS FOUND IN THE BACK OF SEAT 67A

Dear waitress of the air
when you are very old, grey, blind and deaf
disgracing yourself by wetting your tights each time you sneeze or cough
and then breaking wind when you call out in pain and confusion
and when you smell weird as yeast spread and sick
please do tell your meals-on-wheels do-gooder
or help the aged social worker
and indeed your only contact with the outside world
that you once refused to lend a poet a pen
on a short flight to Austria for no reason whatsoever

tell them it was back then, when you were a tangerine coloured air stewardess
with a ballerina bun, a soft fruit fat arse, over plucked eyebrows and liar eyes
tell her how you got quite a little power kick out of the fact you were not
even using it
that biro, right there, in the tippety tip of the top pocket
you were keeping it there to look official
you knew we all knew that you knew that we knew you had spare ones
with the airline name written down the side
in the luxury goods duty-free rip-off trolley
thus forcing the poor dear poet
to write in lipstick on the back of a used sick bag
you understand the poet had a marvellous inspiration upon take off
it could have been the greatest genius of poem of all of our lifetimes
please note that instead of poetry this was what the poet wrote on same
short flight

Dearest sky bar maid
with your halloween pumpkin slit for an inane smile
this one is not for you – you sour faced citrus
but about you – you mottled mandarin skinned reptile

I demand, you bring me ten more vodkas, as I scrawl these words
blurred and smeared, with carroty sick seeping through
I hope that you enjoy a miserable monotonous life
like a one-winged bird going in circles with no real destination or purpose
with your cupreous skin like poor quality leather goods from all that sun-bed
and your jowls sagging from all that hair-bun pinning
stinking of cheap citric acidic perfume
and your arsehole limp from aeroplane fibre-free foodstuff
and all those rough dry arse-rape searches at every landing
I see you baby
I see you with your peach painted talons clinging to an oxygen mask
whilst you lose that very pen to an insane suicidal terrorist madman
who uses it to write his demands on your face mistaking it for an orange post-it
note pad
I hope that pen leaks all over your uniform and dyes your right tit blue
I also hope you choke on rancid pilot sperm

Bon Voyage
Seat 66A

CATHEDRALS

each morning we build cathedrals, we decorate them with sea shells and eyelash salt, warm light and dreams of butterflies.

but by nightfall nothing remains but trampled sand castles, coppery, tarnished green, a fear of the night that drowns us, then the sea that washes it away.

each morning we build cathedrals, we decorate them with gold dust and sea salt kisses, chocolates and silver rings and summer dreams of flying flowers.

but by nightfall nothing remains but a tramp and his dog pissing in winter's doorway, a fear of the fear as the blood of Friday night, washes us away.

each morning we build cathedrals, we decorate them with violet dawn light and dreams of flying, and dreams of dreams of flying.

but by nightfall nothing remains but a list of things to do and a mesh of things unanswered, and the dreadful knowledge that we are not what we intend to do – we are what we already did, intentionally.

and each morning we build cathedrals, this one is made of sandpaper, we decorate it with glitter, phosphorus and ribbons, we ink and hand print our best intentions, we brush it with milk and prick it with a fork and bake it.

by dusk, nothing remains but a rusty caravan, empty balloons are ripped condoms, there's the fear of the plump shadow, and the vodka and the cunts wash all your wishes down, with the laughter like a drain.

this morning you built a cathedral, you rose, you bloomed with prick, kick and thorns, this one has a thick skin of rubber, it will be as soft and yielding as time, forgiving and elastic as love, over and over, again.

THE WONDERMENTALIST

AKA. MATT HARVEY.

WORKS PERKS

…it's just a little thing,
I wouldn't call it pilfering
or petty theft. I took one, yes
but look – there are so many left.
I'm in on time. I smile, work hard.
Why should my conscience twitch or flinch?
Each working week you take a yard,
so why begrudge me my half-inch?

You take the best hours of my day.
What do you give me? Take-home pay.
I'm so tired I can hardly speak –
you take the best days of my week.
You take the best weeks of my month –
I take some paper, this hole-punch.
You take the best months of my year –
I take this swivel-chair. Oh dear.
You take the best years of my life…
… a laminator for the wife

So now please look the other way –
I need my little takeaway
to give myself a token raise
to supplement my take-home praise.

Some get to meet celebrities
or go on junkets overseas
I'm simply taking some of these –
some paper clips, some folder files
a Pritt Stick, stapler, carpet tiles.
Some tippex, a waste-paper bin
this *thing* for putting *thingies* in.
This ream. Okay this box of reams.

This laptop…
…well, you took my *dreams*

How did it ever come to this?
My perky chirpy perquisites
have been turned into exhibits –
these trinkets I gave house-room to:
Exhibits 'A' to 'W'.
Don't ask what reason or what rhyme
drove pretty me to petty crime
nobody's perfect.
I guess it built up over time –
because I'm worth it.

THE PRUNE STONE ORACLE

for practical career prognostication

tinker, tailor, soldier, sailor
affluent, effluent, banker man, brief
drinker, abstainer, personal trainer
rich man, pure man, beauty, beast
   actor, voyeur, pagan priest

starlet, pilot, stylist, harlot
bright spark, damp squib, top dog, dipstick
washer-up, usherette, husher-up, shrink
   chiropractor, astronaut, pimp

ball-girl, cold-caller, wide-boy, kerb-crawler
high-flyer, fall guy, poor cow, small fry
brick-layer, soothsayer, darts player, social worker
   statistician, dietician, fat controller

nobody, somebody, somebody, nobody
pen-pusher, wage-slave, cannon-fodder, dogsbody
magistrate, agitator, high-street prestidigitator
conjuror, registrar, hedge fund manager
   farmer, palmist, media whore

Elvis impersonator, Ofsted inspector
off-white van man, funeral director
busker, wrestler, condom tester
   dowser, rustler, behaviourist, geek

anabolic sports star, bar staff, fraudster
doppelganger look-alike, cock-a-snook porn star
pacifist, panellist, IT specialist
analyst, fetishist, Freudian accountant
butler, bouncer, burglar, minder
  monkey-trainer, organ-grinder

chicken-plucker, puffer-upper, pillow fluffer, blood-sucker
compère, umpire, au pair, vampire
shadow spokesman, identity thief
  doctor
  lawyer
  Indian chief…

PENGE 176

Peter Hayhoe

BUS STOP

Don't snog in front of me

Being the only other person at this bus stop I find it rather uncomfortable

I feel like splitting you two up, and telling you that in a couple of years you'll hate each other, and just the thought of his hand upon your body will make you cringe

And you *Mister*, yes you; you'll be drinking, and screwing girls you currently look down upon because you feel empty and frustrated like everyone else on this shit-awful planet

And maybe at some point you'll bump into one another, and you'll feel really uncomfortable because you won't remember why you got together in the first place
But still you'll be jealous of her boyfriend, gawking like a cocker spaniel next to her

So when you get home you'll text some slut hoping for some phone sex, whilst across town in some seedy bed-sit she'll be doing it for real
Don't worry *son*, she'll feel dirty and unsatisfied just like you

And after a few more years you could be married to different people
But when you're feeding your cherry blossom kids or waxing your vastly expensive car you'll soon realise that your marriage isn't as exciting as that moment beneath the bus stop
And you'll do anything, absolutely anything, to be there again

BROKEN ON THE PILLOW

Those little white pills can't help you, broken on the pillow

And time may heal the wounds somewhat, broken on the pillow

And how fingers grab the edge of sleep as love and loss do finally seep into pools of blindness, broken on the pillow

And maybe I can help you, if only to remain silent and placid, with the right words in the wrong order, broken on the pillow

But like always the old wounds are replaced by the new and I cannot fathom the possibilities of pain and blood

I cannot reach those last few inches between your back and my chest, this little world, broken on the pillow

SUPERMAN

If I were any superhero I would be superman
And sure Superman may seem like an easy answer because he has all the
cool superpowers
He can look through walls or should I say perv
He is almost indestructible apart from kryptonite, which you can't even buy
on eBay nowadays

And he can fly

And this is the super power I am most interested in
Not because it would be quicker to get to the shops or save me money
on holidays to Spain, although that would be a perk
I have no real desire to swoop through the sky or soar like a bird

You see I want to fly because of you

I would circumnavigate around this planet backwards reversing time itself
I would spin and spin and spin this earth until we were but children, grazing
knees, and drinking warm cartons of milk at playtime

I want to be invited over to your birthday party
We can wear paper hats and eat jelly and ice cream
On Saturday mornings you can come over to my house and we can watch
The Raccoons, whilst my mum reheats cans of Alphabetti Spaghetti

And in a few more years I want to stand outside your gate
Me in the black blazer, you in the red
We can argue about who's better, Blur or Oasis
We can share chips outside the kebab shop
We can even go to Croydon, if that's not too forward

I want to be there when we finish school
We can try to get served in pubs and if not the park
We can drink cheap cider and vodka
Eventually one of us will puke
You can rest your head on my lap as we wait for the bus

But I'm rambling
Even if I could turn back time I know it won't be perfect
Things will divide us like people and places and just stuff
We may go to different colleges
We may be involved in different relationships

But I want to be there

I want to be there, for the heartbreaks, and mistakes, and the times, the times
when life just drags you down

And I want to be there at that party, when you first notice something different
about me
When the first seeds of attractions are finally laid
And as the night comes to end
And the last survivors fall blissfully asleep
You look me and realise that I'm not just any man, but your Superman

AN ALIEN ADDRESS

Do you have bendy buses
or are you jet-propelled?
Do you have those things on tube trains,
to be held onto when it's crowded,
I don't know what they're called?
How much is there in your world, that you haven't got
a name for?
Is it the stars that you aim for?
Do you ever get appalled,
when your brand new central heating has been
shoddily installed
by a bunch of cowboys?
Are you green, are you translucent,
do you have any pets?
Do you have mental illness
or menthol cigarettes?
Do you ever feel you don't fit in with all the rest?
Do you feel like an outsider,
like a money spider in a nest
of penniless termites?
Do you ever say 'To be honest'?
Do you ever say 'For my sins'?
Or are truthfulness and repentance where another
world begins?
Do your bins get emptied on a Tuesday?
Do you have three-legged races
you can compete in on your own?
Do you have a stripy deck chairs that get wind blown
when they're vacant?
Is there anybody out there?
Have you got ears for this?
Have you got liver tablets,
or the equivalent of Bristol?

Do you wear a pair of glasses, for maybe you
        have eyes?
Do you start off as a baby and then increase in size,
but lose your sense of wonderment in the process?
Do you ever get on a crowded train
and have to put your luggage in the vestibule
and do you ever sit in the seat nearest the door
so you can keep an eye on it
and then more people get on
and you have to stand up and say
'Excuse me, but could you move out the way, please,
I cannot see my luggage'?

TAKING OUT THE 'IN IT' AND PUTTING 'INNIT' IN IT

This clock has still got a lot of mileage in it.
This clock is well-stocked with mileage, innit.

This society has still got deep class divisions in it.
Classwise, this society is still deeply divided, innit.

This potato has the possibility of the most delightful
    bloom in it.
This potato is bloomful of possible delight, innit.

This gap between the floorboards has got some little
    bits of old cheese in it.
Have you thought about doing some hoovering, innit.

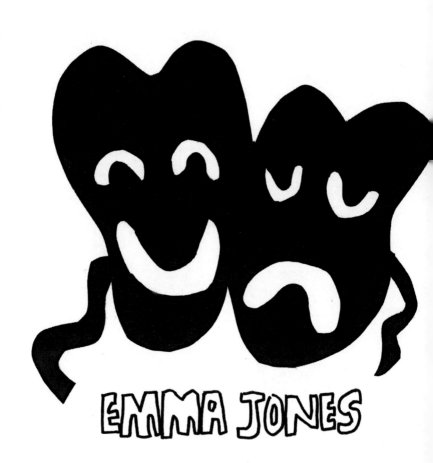

EMMA JONES

GCSE

Miss you're always on about GCSEs
Oh gosh, you should allow it Miss please
It just seems so singular
There's more important fings you knaa

G.C.S.E.
Like:
Girls
Cussing
Shadika's
Extensions
Cause oh my days Miss, did I mention?
That thing on her head looked flammable
It was like a dead flippin' animal!
I lie? True say I don't chat shit
It wasn't a weave it was more like a thatch, yeah?

G.C.S.E.
Miss! I gotta GCSE!
I've got to Get to the Chicken Shop... Early!
I promised Devontae I'd buy him some hot wings
And Miss I've got to cause he's such a hot ting
I'm gonna meet wiv him, eat wiv him, maybe later b...
Anyway Miss, I've gotta boost fam!
N' don't cut your eyes at me cause that's the truth man!

G.C.S.E.
Miss...
I've got to Get to College Somewhere Eventually
and I've got to Get my Core Subjects like English
And I've got to Get my Coursework Sent to the Examiners
Mister Manufor told me dis dis morning,
And Miss! I can't just ignore him

And no disrespect Miss,
And don't get vexed Miss, but:
It's just drama. It's just drama.

Miss I've gotta GCSE!
Gotta get Chung for the Shubs this Eve!
I'm gonna look swaggalicious all in purple
I can't stay for no after school rehearsal
And anyway
I don't like this play;
It's... Gay.....

Miss you're always on about GCSEs
Oh gosh, you should allow it Miss please
It just seems so singular
There's more important fings you knaa!

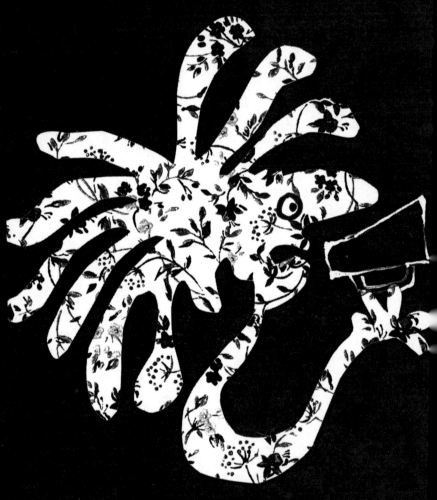

Murray Lachlan Young

MAGGIE: OBIT POEM

Farewell to you Maggie Oh Maggie farewell
Some eulogise you, some give you hell
Repeating the phrases that caused notoriety
Stating there is no such thing as society

Friend to the bank, brutally frank
Reagan's big pal, rode in a tank
You mobilised classes with social volte-faces
You mangled the unions, kicked euro arses

Maggie, Maggie, Maggie!

You parleyed with Pinochet, gifted the satirist.
Nelson Mandela, you branded a terrorist
Flogged council houses, sold the utilities
Founded new Labour in all probability

One usually lost if one stood up and fought yer
You hammered your colleagues like lambs to the slaughter

Stated the Falklands were 'ours' in totality
Turned the big bang to a fiscal reality
Littered the city with monstrous earning
The lady you stated was never for turning

Your standing it seems in the final prognosis
Reviled and admired in similar doses
Some will remember the chill in your air
Some will remember your teeth and your hair

But most that you gave and you asked for no quarter

Maggie, Maggie, Maggie!

Over and out

But not bad for a greengrocer's daughter

MURRAY LACHLAN YOUNG

ELVIS M^cGONAGALL

YOU CAN
CALL ME DAVE

Change, Optimism, Hope
Progress, Energy, Vigour
Modest, Moderate, Modern
Brighter, Better, Bigger

Conservative, Compassionate, Liberal
Black, Muslim, Gay
Young, Green, Martian
Work, Rest, Play

Responsible, Tangible, Real
Motivation, Dedication, Aspiration
Empower, Enhance, Improve
Location, Location, Location

Freedom, Wealth, Opportunity
Courage, Resolve, Expertise
Beliefs, Values, Dreams
Eats, Shoots, Leaves

On, My, Bike
Eco, Friendly, Guy
Recycle, Renew, Relax
Take, Off, Tie

Liberty, Equality, Paternity
Women, Babies, Men
Co-operation, Coalition, Cocaine?
Never, Ever, Again

ELVIS McGONAGALL

Trusting, Caring, Sharing
Rebekah, Rupert, Andy
Emerson, Lake, Palmer
Yankee, Doodle, Dandy

Beanz, Meanz, Heinz
Ready, Steady, Go
Leg, Before, Wicket
Edgar, Allen, Poe

Mary, Mungo, Midge
Beverly, Hills, Cop
Yabba, Dabba, Doo
Snap, Crackle, Pop

Keep, It, Real
Watch, Me, Blog
Pimp, My, Ride
Snoop, Doggie, Dogg

Boo, Ya, Shaka
In, Da, Hood
Super, Smashing, Great
Finger, Lickin', Good

Suit, You, Sir
Are, Friends, Electric?
Want, That, One
Vorsprung, Durch, Technik

ELVIS McGONAGALL

Bloody, Nice, Bloke
Sun, Shiney, Day
Blobby, Blobby, Blobby
Gabba, Gabba, Hey

Drivel, Piffle, Bilge
Yackety, Yack, Yack
Rhubarb, Rhubarb, Rhubarb
Quack, Quack, Quack

Silver, Spoon, Face
Chubby, Puppy, Fat
Shiny, Wavy, Hair
Notting, Hill, Twat

Same, Old, Tory
Eton, Blood, Blue
Brand, New, Package
Blair, Mark, Two

IF... (with apologies to Mr Kipling)

If you can keep your daddy's trust fund while all about you
Are losing homes and jobs and blaming it on you
If you can dream of a day when compassion is taboo
When wellbeing belongs to the complacent few
If you can wear your arrogance and greed like cheap cologne
If you can smoke cigars rolled on poverty's thigh
If being born to rule Britannia is bred in your bone
If you can lasso power with your old school tie

If you can spread a little privilege to those in need
But let the undeserving paupers eat Pedigree Chum
If you can give to a charity like Children In Tweed
But still sneer at scurvy scroungy benefit scum
If you put the boot into those shameless shirking skivers
But you can pay yourself a bonus and not laugh
If you can hymn the praises of the hard working strivers
And grovel on your knees before the golden calf

If your underpants are handmade from gilded ocelot
If your suit is cut from the cloth of others' pain
If you can knock back martinis on an oligarch's yacht
And buy a ticket for the corporate gravy train
If you can spend each weekend in your stately country pile
If your smooth pink well-fed cheeks tend towards the flabby
If you think comedy means Boris dancing Gangnam Style
And the apogee of art is Downton Abbey

If you believe that bolshie Marxists run the BBC
And tax avoidance is a perk of the elite
If you can take the sugar out of someone else's tea
And transform NHS into New Harley Street
If you can really milk the system for all that it's worth
If you know you've won the race before it's even run
Then – you'll have the whole world in your wallet, yours is the Earth
And – you'll be a selfish Tory bastard my son

ELVIS McGONAGALL

AN ANALYSIS OF THE EFFECTS UPON THE ARTS OF THE COLLAPSE OF AN UNFETTERED FREE-MARKET RISK-PRONE, PRIVATISED, PROFIT-DRIVEN, GREEDY-BASTARD TURBO-CAPITALIST ECONOMIC SYSTEM AND THE CONCOMITANT ECONOMIC POLICY OF DEFICIT REDUCTION AND NEO-LIBERAL AUSTERITY MEASURES

Times are hard
Belts are tight
Cupboards are empty
Pockets are light
Cuffs are frayed
Nerves are fraught
Cuts are deep
Poems are short

THE QUEEN'S SPEECH

My government will meet the aspirations of the nation
Introducing legislation to promote regeneration

Who writes this stuff? It's so mundane
It's my speech – let's start again

Word up you commoners, serfs and tramps
I'm that woman from off of the stamps

Yo! Rule Brittannia! Sing Hosanna!
Don't anybody dare mention Diana

I'm the pearly queen, I'm England's rose
You's my bitches, you's my ho's

Castles, palaces, livin' it large
Diamond-studded golden barge

21st century Cleopatra
Bessie in da big house comin' at ya

Floating up the Thames in a royal flotilla
Why's that horse in a hat? Oh no – it's Camilla

Curtsy, bow, kowtow, grovel
Fly a little flag from your ghastly hovel

Flap those tea-towels, swing from the bunting
Pour me a gin – let's go hunting

We're the Windsor posse one cannot quarrel
Shoot some peasants at Balmoral

ELVIS McGONAGALL

(Terribly sorry that should be "pheasants" not "peasants" – Freudian slip)

I got the guns, I got the bling
The Prince of Biscuits will never be king

Prince Will.i.am is the family mascot
Hats on homies let's big it up at Ascot

Fo shizzle my nizzle – pardon one's French
We diss Helen Mirren and Judi Dench

I'm Her Majesty – they're absurd
Give me an Oscar – I'm James Bond's bird

Cut some ribbons, shake some hands
Sit through another boring military band

Wave, wave, wave, wave, wave
Wave, wave, wave, wave, wave

Oh Christ! Cliff Richard! Pass the paracetemol
Bring on the dancing corgis – so much better LOL

And don't complain about the language –
It's my fucking English – have another sandwich

Build me a yacht, roast me a swan
Bring me the head of bloody Elton John

Behold my crown – see it dazzle
Prince Harry says Andrew's a bit of a vajazzle

Get down with the youth, ignore all syntax
Like, y'know, whatever, everybody chillax

Just sack a few butlers in times of austerity
One never cared for Burrell – far too ferrety

Headscarf, tweeds and a sensible brogue
Don't just stand there Philip – c'mon vogue!

Cheer up Broken Britain, it's my jubilee
God won't help you – he's busy saving me

The Bard of Barnsley

TONY BOUGHT A GUITAR AND GOT A PARKING FINE

This happened in Retford. Trains pass
Through Retford at speed but Tony and I
Had time to kill. Charity shops. A café
Where the silvery teapot reflected my face.

Another charity shop. I flicked through
Paperbacks: Gervase Phinn, Captain Corelli.
But Tony saw the guitar. Oh, Tony, surely
Not? But he did. And by now it was ten past two.

We rushed. His guitar twanged in the air.
We got back to the car just too late, too late.
Tony shouted. There was unseasonal heat
For October. He flung the ticket to the Retford floor

And I opened my mouth and said a daft thing
And my face turned red in the afternoon sun.
First silvery. Now red. Trains pass through. They're gone.
Tony flailed at the strings in a heartbroken song.

Tony kippered the strings in a heartbroken song.
Tony rinsed out the strings in heartbroken song.
Tony light-greened the strings in a heartbroken song.
Tony teatowelled the strings in a heartbroken song.

MATHEMATICS

He says,

Those goddamn Pakistanis and their goddamn corner shops
Built a shop on every corner took our British workers' jobs
He says those goddamn Chinese and their goddamn china shops
I tell him they're from Vietnam but he doesn't give a toss
I ask him what was there before that damn Japan man's shop
He stares at me and dreams a scene of British workers' jobs
Of full time full employment before the goddamn boats all came
Where everybody went to work full time every day
A British Business stood there first he claims before the Irish came
Now British people lost their jobs and bloody Turkish are there to blame
I ask him how he knows that fact he says because it's true
I ask him how he *knows* the fact he says he read it in the news
Everytime a Somalian comes here they take a job from us
The mathematics one for one, from us to them it just adds up
He bites his cake and sips his brew and says again he knows the spot
The goddamn Carribeans came and now good folk here don't have jobs
I ask him what was there before the goddamn Persian curtain shop
I show him architecture plans of empty goddamn plots of land
I show him the historic maps
A bit of sand a barren land
There was no goddamn shop before those Pakistanis came and planned man
I'm sick of crappy mathematics
Cos I love a bit of sums
I spent three years into economics
And I geek out over calculus
And when I meet these paper claims
That one of every new that came
Takes away one's daily wage
I desperately want to scream
"your maths is stuck in primary"
Cos some who come here also spend

And some who come here also lend
And some who come here also tend
To set up work which employs them
And all your balance sheets and trends
Work with numbers not with men
And all your goddamn heated talk
Ignores the trade the Polish brought
Ignores the men they gave work to
Not just plumbing jobs but further too
Ignores the ones they buy stock from
Accountants, builders, on and on
And I know it's nice to have someone
To blame our lack of jobs upon
But immigration's not as plain
Despite the sums inside your brain
As one for one, as him or you
As if he goes, they'll employ you
Cos sometimes one that comes makes two
And sometimes one can add three more
And sometimes two times two is much much more
Than four
And most times immigrants bring more
Than minuses

WILLIES ARE MORE DANGEROUS THAN GUNS

I learnt this from censorship, the government, films and television.

Willies are much more dangerous than guns.

Especially when the owner of that willy has a hard'un.

So I just don't understand what I must've missed or if there's something about a man's bits I haven't quite understood.

'Cause we ban penises on TV as if they're some magic concoction to turn teenagers into

sex addicts and kill all children who watch them, as if the sight of this six-inch slug

between a man's thighs could burn down family ties and destroy peoples' lives.

I know men call it their magic wand but it's really not that powerful,

a little tool to wave around it's really not that bountiful

and they might call it their cannon, but it's really not that large

and the cannon balls it sometimes shoots out really aren't that hard

and as soldiers go, as I've heard it called, it's just a little weak

'cause even when it's stood to attention it's normally ready to sleep.

But still.

Willies are more dangerous than guns.

Even when shooting blanks they are our enemy number one, so I just don't understand what

I must be missing or if there's something about a man's bits I haven't quite got a grip on yet.

'Cause as we pollute, loot and shoot British bullets into blazing nights

we teach our children that this piece of skin is a more frightening sight than dropping bombs

on children in Iraq like sick falling sweets, selling weapons worldwide waging war on the weak.

While we burn down more forest to produce more fake needs,

spill oil into seas, spread disease and kill species

TVs and we teach our children that Rambo and Van Damme are cool

but a boy with an erection is a 'sick and dirty fool',

that that man on the hot bus with an uncontrollable, embarrassing lift is
not a biological
twitch but a 'sick old pervie git'.
We pay for plastic guns and water pistols to entertain our kids
but under absolutely no circumstance let them see a dick.
We stare at bloody bodies bullets broken bones and starving kids
but banned from seeing naked bodies: male or female 'special' bits.
I know I must be missing something 'cause otherwise it seems a little silly
to teach people they can play with guns but not with their own willies.
The government's most censored image. Our public enemy number one.
Please, tell me what I'm missing
if willies
are more dangerous
than guns.

D.I.L.F.

Since I've seen him change a nappy it seems his penis has grown,
muscles made more pronounced each time he folds those babygros.
His thighs were pretty buff before but since he's laid her on the floor,
one foot rocking her to sleep, the other touching toes with me
it seems his thighs are like three thousand times as juicy now.
Since I've seen him
push a pram
cook a meal with kid in hand
concoct a song to rock-a-bye
wake to cries with smiling eyes
pit stop challenge
changing kicks
cleaning rags of baby sick,
since I've seen him doing it
it seems his bits are twice as big, his lips are twice as ripe to kiss,
his neck nape twice as nice to lick.
I just have half the time to do it.
Since we've had a kid.

ADRIAN MEALING

THREE POINTS ON MY LICENCE

Driving through Cambridge, it's dark and it's late
back from the airport and I'm in a state
pop goes the camera, bang goes the gun
I'm speeding, didn't see it and I'm over the ton

three points on the doormat, give to the wife
marital coercion, no, she's sharp as a knife
you could cut your finger on her, on my life
three points on my licence? No, gone to the wife

I'm a civil servant, married to Chris
now he's playing away and I don't need this
a ring and a promise, three kids on my knee
three points for speeding, he gave to me

I'll talk to the papers, get him into court
show him I'm a woman who can't be bought
it's the end of our road and I'm on a mission
turn left up ahead, it's not my coalition

three points on my licence, give 'em back with interest
marital coercion? Kiss my tea-chest
slice the man in two, a liar through and through
perjury, perjury, now who's in the stew?

three points on the doormat, give to the wife
marital coercion, no, she's sharp as a knife
you could cut your finger on her, on my life
three points on my licence? No, gone to the wife

Think twice, think twice, before you do
Think of your family before you think of you
I wish I had that fatal day
Three points on the doormat came to stay

EARLHAM CEMETERY NOVEMBER

A knock-off iPod in my pocket
I jog among the sadly missed.
It's not just autumn leaves that stun, but
the best-kept graves I've ever seen.

Tattoos aren't really permanent
sand was once proud rock
everything you've said is gone
and that dusty smell in books is rot.

I fell for a drowning man once.
Watched him walk to the sea from the shore.
As his outstretched hand slipped under,
I'd never loved him more.

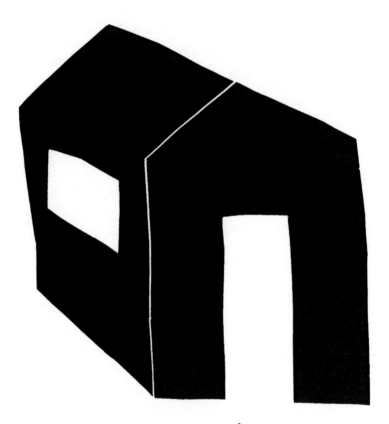

JOHN OSBORNE'S
SHED.

OUR WAITRESS IS EMPLOYEE OF THE MONTH

Her photograph is in the foyer
and I imagine her pretending not to be bothered
when it was announced at the team meeting
a semi-circle of applause.

But the next morning she'd have shown her mum
the Twenty Pound High Street Voucher
and her mum would have said "Well done," and meant it,
because she knows it's important
to appreciate the small things.

And in town our waitress will have gone from shop to shop
content she didn't have to start work until half seven that evening.
Trying on a maxi dress in River Island
she'd wonder whether it was for the time
she helped an amputee cut up his food

managing to strike the perfect balance between being too fussy
and pretending she hadn't noticed.
She didn't even need to say anything like
"Shall I help you with that?"

it was just this intuition
she didn't even realise she had
and as she helped chop up his gammon and potatoes
he told her he was in town to see his daughter

who had just proposed to her boyfriend
taking advantage of the leap year
and he was so nervous he wouldn't get on with his future son-in-law.
Our waitress would have asked if he'd like a dessert,

and at first he'd have said no
but she'd have said "Oh, go on!"
because she knows it's important to appreciate the small things.
She'd have smiled as he scooped up the last of his custard.

Our table is ready. The four of us take our seats
and as she hands out the menus
puts serviettes on our knees, she must know that we know,
we'd been in the foyer for so long, staring at her photograph

and I think: Please, no-one say anything,
don't let it be like the time we saw Dame Judi Dench
get out of a taxi by the Old Vic and shouted Judi, Judi
like paparazzi
until she turned and waved so awkwardly.

Let's just be grateful we're being served by the Employee of the Month
and as she carries our plates of seabass
we know that if any of us start to choke on a bone
we will feel her arm around us.

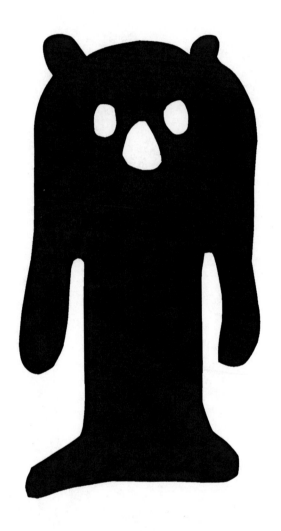

POLARBEAR.

ORANGE

The year 9 boy stares at me. Like he's convinced
the answer is hidden in my face.
His eyes twitch. I can almost hear his brain working.
His mate digs his arm and
tells him to forget it, that nothing
rhymes with orange.
I smile. He refuses to give up.
Their young teacher shouts over that we need to
finish our pieces and not to worry about the rhyme.
While the rest of the class get on
with their work I lean
on the boy's table and tell him that if he wants
to take the whole session's time
trying to rhyme the word orange, I'm alright with that and to make sure he shows me
what he comes up with.
His mate asks me if I've noticed how when I'm just
speaking out loud normally it's like
I'm rhyming, a few others agree.
I smile and tell him I don't know
what he's talking about but, how sometimes, when I'm just walking about, a
thought will come out and before I know what I'm doing I'm sorting it out into
a pattern, to the point where nothing else matters even when I'm crossing the
road and about to be flattened by a bus, I can't rush an idea and I know that
might sound like I'm quite weird but maybe it's kinda like when a drummer
stands in the queue at the bank and without even knowing starts tapping a beat
with his hand and his feet and the other people notice and start to focus on
the rhythm and that there are so many patterns in the way that we speak in the
cadence and spaces between, how we breathe, our intonation not to mention
emphasis and the gentle inflective differences cos everyone of us has our own
way of speaking that carries a unique way of reaching out to other people and if
that's what he means?

I dunno sir. I just thought you were rapping ennit.

~~MOTHER TERESA~~
~~SHIRLEY TEMPLE~~
~~SIMON TEMPLAR~~
~~TINIE TEMPAH~~
KATE TEMPEST

PARABLES

At last we watch these cities topple.
We knew this beast would eat itself.
It feasts itself into digestion,
shitting us out in a mess of rejected intestines,
but we weakly willed
cry tears when we hear that the beast is killed.

Each has spilled themselves before it,
begged this beast to eat its fill.

People still believe that their rewards will come,
That's why they're keeping still.

Heeding the shrill pitch of its persuasion,
living each day for the next temptation.

We extended the invitation,
we coaxed the beast down from the hills,
we said – come.
Come, wreck our hearts,
come fill our hands with wealth
and don't show no mercy
– ah, but the beast it fooled us,
told us it loved us
when really it ruled us,
subtly screwed us
all down into place,
while we wept in its name
and begged for a taste.

It sung us into sphinx like comas,
now friendly faces have turned paranoid loners,
we knelt at its feet and worshipped what owned us,
it charmed us so it could dethrone us.

These are the times of the parables.
These are the times
of the freeborn minds self-manacled.
The times prophesied by the ancients,
when the days are so full
that they've made us vacant.

When it's all so easy to grab
we get complacent,
our senses defenceless against the invasion
of hostile forces parading as friendly.
We got so much
that it left us empty.
So we got more in a frenzy
to fill up the void
but the void keeps increasing.
it seems we're all speaking so much
we've lost meaning,
it seems we're all deep in the guts
of a demon.

This ain't no overblown theory,
I'm not saying this is the work of some secret pact,
I'm saying – this is the outcome
of consumer identity,
that is the beast at our back.

And it has the support of the courts and the law,
so now we can't trust justice,
she feeds the beast's jaws
with the bodies that writhe
in a heap on the floor,
and now the jails are all flooded with the blood of the poor.

We must be like the water,
head back to the source,
instead we're grinning away while the rot rocks our core,
but what for?
our smiles are locked doors
and hearts are not sure
that we even want more,
the meaning of mine isn't mine anymore,
it's 'not yours',
but still I maintain, we are not a lost cause.

These are the times of the parables.
These are the times
of the freeborn minds self-manacled.
The times prophesied by the ancients,
when the days are so full
that they've made us vacant.

So just love.
Be filled with love
and have strength enough
to be still when shoved.
The filth and rust
can't corrupt
the goodness that fills your blood,
and all truth is built on trust,
and it's up to us to move right,
coz moves must get made,
so be bare faced in this masquerade,
too many hearts have greyed
in the dullness of days
but our hearts are displayed
as we charge on like it's the last parade,

we don't believe that we can't be saved
we believe in change
and we believe it transpires when we need it,
but the ships that we sail are not sea fit,
these vessels,
filled with the chaos of commerce
are what's leading us into the wreckage.

But we're at the helm though,
we've got the tiller in hand
and the truth that was lost
we can still understand,
we need to build bridges over this splintered land,
before the hourglass cracks
and it spills its sand.

These are the times of the parables.
These are the times
of the freeborn minds self-manacled.
The times prophesied by the ancients,
when the days are so full
that they've made us vacant.

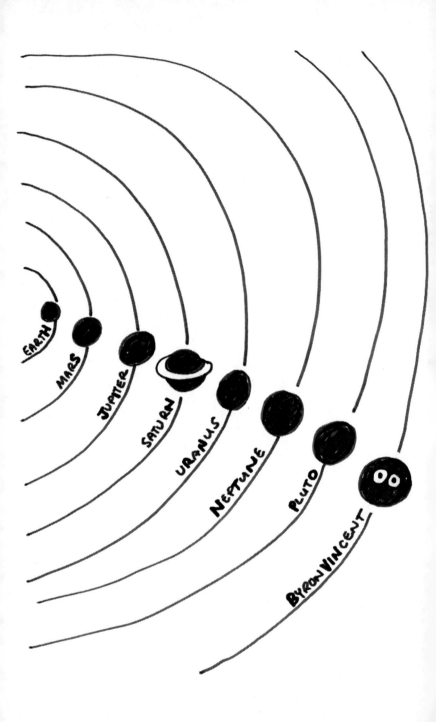

NEWSROTIC

Hello, good evening and shut up.
Dramatic synthesizer music
Like sobs of ZX Spectrum's schizophrenic ghost.
Techno cynic does Krav Maga on your silly heart.

Good evening, OR IS IT?
Text in with your opinions.
I tanned middle aged man
I expensive tie serious.
I hint of regional accent so proles do trust,
but not so much offends Berkshire.

I monotone truth wizard.
You listen good now.

MP licks semi-aquatic mammal for sex fun.
Opposition call to outlaw man glands
"Dotter, dotter, dirty otter,
dotter, dotter, otter botty"
Claims bestiologist Dr Humpty McMuley

New urban youth craze 'Tickle stabbing'.
Codgers beware. More on that later.

Bad thing in hot place, text in with awful poetry.

Obesity in wasps hits epidemic proportions. More on that later.

Theoretical Kruggerands eaten by hedge fund or fun hedge or hedgehogs or
something.
You move into old fridge and eat offal from buckets now.
Steal contents of child's piggy bank and spend on Buckfast.
Text in with pathetic fears, sofa maggots.

This just in:
Germs breeding in the grubby weft of your happy blanket.

Young attractive female anchor reads tweet
"Barry from Colchester says something reactionary."
Three waves of feminism mocked by pigs' trotters in matching neckties.
Nothing on that later.

TERROR!
You feel quiver botty now.
Disconcerting non-European beards.
THREATENING MAP GRAPHIC!
Vowels and consonants arranged in different order to that of which you're
used to.
This just in:
Terror bad, should probs start war against it or something.
Text in with latent racism.

This just in:
War against abstract concept unwinnable.
Text in with ill-informed dunderheaded twottery.

THIS NOW!
Overseas contingency news.
"We're contingencying the crap out of Iraqisbeckistan or wherever."
claims Whitehouse word moron,
moron…
More on that later.

This just in:
Navy seals assassinate Terror Hawks, just in case.
Navy seals assassinate terrapins, same reason.
Navy seals assassinate Terry Nutkins.
Claim find subliminal Jihadi subtext in old episodes of Really Wild Show.
You hide in womb built of flak jackets and paranoia now.

Gap year twonk head-butting Tescos,
more sexy news good than reasoned debate.
You like this.
We show again,
and again,
and again…

You punch own rational perspective in thorax now.

Greased tripe in sequined thong wows dingbats.
"Look at the shiny lies." Says Max Clifford.
Max Clifford's existence, all your fault.
You loathe self now.
Go on,
loathe self.
It's more than you deserve.

Something emotionally exploitative,
text in with tedious indignation.

Market research company looks on twitter then tells PR lizard to tell oleaginous
politician to tell us the thing that we're now telling you.
"I like that thing that's trending." Claims snake eyed git weasel.

And Finally…

User generated guff of cow trapped in Renault Espace
Smile now, idiots.
I've been consistently indifferent.
Don't have nightmares.
Good night.

ZOOM!

The bonnet is a shield protecting you from the modern sickness; its lines are the supreme creation of an era.

The headlights are the meticulous eyes of the first robot looking into the future from the past.

The exhaust is a sardonic goodbye.

The boot is the old suitcase in which you keep a well-thumbed copy of your escape fantasy.

The bumper is a cut-throat razor that has never been opened; the threat of it alone is enough.

The chrome trim is Connery as Bond, skiing down the volcanic slopes of a villain's lair.

The FM radio is a telegram, agreeing with your disappointment at the state of things.

The antenna is a 1955 Gibson Super 400 archtop.

The fuel tank is a single malt in your father's stomach.

The door handles are rabbit holes leading to adventure.

The angles are your first crush or notes in a perfect chord.

The doors are your boyhood self as batman.

The windows are a private screening of your favourite film.

The indicators are a civil 'excuse me' in a theme-pub brawl.

The odometer is the best anecdote you've ever heard.

The speedometer is a beckoning index finger.

The ignition is a toe dipped in the sea.

The sparkplug is a popping cork.

The hubcaps are rose tinted mirrors.

The engine is a cheering crowd or the blind leap between lust and love.

The horses that power it are more mythical than bestial; they chain smoke Marlboros and take long lunches whenever they like.

The hydraulics are a boy showing off to his big brother.

The dashboard is the face of a benevolent alien god.

The steering wheel is a tossed coin that always lands in your favour.

The passenger seat is an invitation.
The driver's seat is a time machine.
The day is an unwritten to do list.
The sunset is your sat nav.
The accelerator is your favourite song.
The road is a Choose Your Own Adventure book.
The rear view mirror is filled with things that can wait.
Ahead of you there is nothing, or everything, whatever you prefer.

SONNET TO THE CYNICAL

This is a sonnet to the cynical. It's technically not even a sonnet.
It's a heart shaped box of cyanide chocolates, but more whimsical, because it
hates consumerism but likes hugs
and its cynicism comes from a good place – a place that says,
"I love you...
with all my garage flowers!"

It's that after hours, after thought, aftertaste of hasty confectionery.
It's, "You bought a teddy with a heart on it
and you'll have to live with that for the rest of your life man!"
"Don't lecture me!...

...I'm sensitive."

This is a call out to those who'd fall out over nothing, rather than sit through
one more viewing of Twilight. A Fight Night on the scrabble tiles...
"No, I don't think it'll be in the dictionary.
You think it might be an exotic bird? An I-hat-eyou? No it's...I HATE you...
Awkward!"

This is the tree with the message
'Happy Commercially Orchestrated Romance Day' carved into the bark
'cause *actual* trees trump recycled cards
and yes they do like a balloon shaped like a heart but not an actual aorta.
Worst present ever apparently.

This is not a sonnet to poets who know that this is NOT a sonnet.
This is a sonnet to the cynical.
The clinical removal of the tear glands. Banned substances include perfume,
massage oils and aftershave.
This is a conviction to P D A –

(Public Displays of Affliction)
It doesn't actually **want** a kiss and even if you **had** a kiss it wouldn't **want** it...

unless you were fit or somefink.

Ring a ring of roses
BOOM!
You know there's a mushroom cloud blooming behind your eyes,
threatening to burst through the top of your head and destroy this room,
but instead...
Nothing.
No tables burst into flames. No flesh is stripped from bone.
No one sees or feels the words you just received on your phone.

This is a sonic boom sonnet to the cynical. The quizzical look that demands,
"Tell me something LESS romantic
than a designated day for romance?"

LUKE WRIGHT.

NIGEL FARRIDGE

The National Front in Barbour jackets
raise a haunchy thigh then slap it!
Vaudeville meets British Legion,
keen as mustard *(Not the Dijon!)*
blight upon our rural regions.
Frigg-orf Froggies! Bog-orf Bosch!
The EDL with shot of posh
sect of hogwash, cult of tosh
Cool-aid? No! It's lemon squash!
Gouty chaps in first class carriage
drum your guts for Nigel Farridge!

Cream-stuffed cat with verbal squits
who's banging on about the Blitz
and stoic wives in ration queues:
All gusto, guts and thrifty stews.
And that, he says, is what we'll lose
if Europe gets its way much more:
Bring back inches! Bring back war!
Polish Plumbers – there's the door!
Repatriate our ancient laws
and let's annul the Brussels marriage!
Morris dance for Nigel Farridge.

Who makes the likes of Gove and Hunt
seem worthy of a poll booth punt,
who headline grabs and steers debate
towards this fabled super-state
then claims he gives it to us straight.
And meanwhile, as this nonsense drones,
this cod-lament for tea and scones,
we're drowning under pay-day loans
with Tories picking at our bones.
A ruddy, fuddy-duddy barrage
flog the wogs it's Nigel Farridge!

Who seems to think that if he's nattish
you won't spot his inner-fascist.
Middle-Brits, he thinks you're dense
with purple placards on your fence
he lies and calls it common sense:
Conserve, conserve keep Britain free
and hug it till it cannot breathe.
I know you all agree with me,
he carps despite his NO MPs.
We must protect our sovereignty.
As if we ever had any!
Here's a truth, so write it large:
we plebs will never be in charge
by cheering blue-blood like Farage.

LUKE WRIGHT

DRAW YOUR PORTRAIT
HERE ↓

YOUR NAME HERE

POEM TITLE HERE

WRITE POEM HERE ↗

WRITE YOUR POEM HERE

WRITE YOUR POEM HERE